MW01601498

Standing on the Sho

©Copyright 2022 Alexander Cowan, Rev

Kindle Direct Publishing

ISBN: 9798386233372

Alexander Cowan

Skyland Baptist Church
3320 Skyland Boulevard East
Tuscaloosa, Alabama 35405

CONTENTS

Foreword   v

Introduction   xi

1. The Mission   1

    Jerome Stancil Robinson   2

    The First Service   4

    The 30,000 Movement   7

2. To God be the Glory   17

    Sanctuary Renovation   18

    Worship Leadership   22

    Revival   24

    The First Retirement   27

3. We're Gonna Win   37

    Jimmy's Early Years   37

    Jimmy Arrives   24

    Jimmy's Team   44

4. Jimmy, Jim, and Jon   51

    Jim Young   51

    The Death of Jerome   53

Jon Wiggins   55

Faith and Katrina   57

Jimmy Interviews   58

The Second Retirement   62

  5. Conclusion   73

FOREWORD

As the current Senior Pastor at Skyland Baptist Church, it is a joy to reflect back on the faithfulness of the members of Skyland Baptist Church over the past 60 years. It's an incredible. blessing to serve as pastor of this church. Alex Cowan has done a masterful job of retelling the incredible story of our church family. As you read, you will hear stories based on interviews and historical documents.

They will tell a story of God's astounding grace, displayed in the lives of many men and women who made great sacrifices for the glory of God. Many of these people in these pages have received their heavenly rewards and are with the Lord. However, we still have some active members today who were members when Skyland went from being a mission to an established church. Over the past six decades, there have been highs and lows. Nevertheless, Skyland Baptist Church continues to be an enormous blessing to the community of East Tuscaloosa.

Culture and Methods of Ministry Often Change

"We live in a different world now," is a phrase often spoken when a great deal of change occurs in how people live their lives from one generation to the next. Certainly, the culture of the 1960's and 2020's seem worlds apart. Only a decade ago in the U.S. 75% of people described themselves as Christian. That number went down to 63% in 2022. In 2019, 34% of people said they were regular church goers. That number dropped to 28% in just two years. There are less people claiming to be Christians and less people going to church. Nonetheless, Skyland Baptist continues to be a light in the darkness. Since 2020 (the year of the Covid pandemic), our church has moved toward our community in a few strategic ways.

Firstly, we began to grow a connection with a local elementary school. Our Treehouse ministry picks up about 50 children (age five to twelve) every week from the school and brings them to church. We feed them, do homework, share Jesus, and love on these children. Recently, I baptized a parent of one of the children that we pick up each week. She came to church for a few weeks prior to her coming forward to trust in Jesus as her Savior and Lord.

Secondly, we started a ministry called Families Count. This ministry exists to help parents that have lost their children to DHR or are in jeopardy of losing their children to DHR. We have the opportunity to teach these parents basic life skills, with a Christ-centered curriculum produced by Lifeline Children's Services. Our volunteers help teach the curriculum, provide transportation as needed, serve as mentors, and prepare a meal each week. God is using this ministry to restore broken families in our community with the hope of the gospel.

Lastly, with the decline in attendance caused by Covid, many sister churches in Tuscaloosa County were struggling. In five years, the amount of Tuscaloosa County Baptist Association churches went from 76 to 68. Therefore, I started a pastor's cohort to help train lay men in our church to be able to preach a sermon. My hope was to be able to provide preaching for struggling churches for about two months. During the two months, the church could facilitate difficult conversations about how the Lord might be leading them in the future. In just a couple of years we have been able to support and encourage close to ten churches.

The Gospel We Proclaim Does Not Change

Skyland Baptist Church is firmly committed to reaching people with the gospel (the good news of Jesus Christ). The gospel is summed up in the doing, dying, and rising of Jesus Christ. Jesus lived a sinless life in perfect obedience to the Father. He then took the punishment we deserved at the cross, dying in our place as the perfect sacrifice for sin. Finally, he rose in powerful victory over sin and death. We believe the gospel proclaimed from scripture changes people: it resurrects hearts, removes idolatry, and restores lives. Families are restored, neighborhoods are renewed, and whole cities are transformed by its power.

Thus, we preach the gospel. We counsel with the gospel. We celebrate the gospel in song. We remember the gospel by partaking in the Lord's Supper. We learn to live in light of the gospel in every sphere of life. From our personal lives, to our homes, to our neighborhoods, to the schools and vocations we take in this city, to the ends of the earth; this community in word and deed will proclaim the good news of a Risen Savior until he comes for us his bride.

Jon Wiggins

April 17th, 2023

x |

INTRODUCTION

"Many small people, who in many small places do many small things, can alter the face of the world."

Alvai & Rauox

I have always had a passion for history. Especially, how the actions of the past shape the reality of the present. Although written in the Spring of 2023, this book will focus on the time from 1963 – 2016. These years encapsulate the ministries of the first two pastors, Jerome Robinson and Jimmy Garner. This book is imperfect and does not tell the whole story of Skyland Boulevard Baptist Church. Words will never fully describe God's faithfulness to this congregation. However, I think it best to at least attempt.

I wish to thank those who have recorded our church history. This book relied heavily upon the bulletins, directories, and accounts safe-guarded by previous generations. I desire this book to serve as a historical foundation from which future generations can build upon. May there be many editions in the years to come.

Jerome, our first pastor, wrote the history of Mt. Olive Baptist, which he pastored. Reading the Preface, I discovered we both deeply love church history. I share Jerome's perspective when he wrote, "I have constantly searched old records to know more about the church. I have thought for a long time I would like to write the history of the church, but was always a little reluctant to attempt it. I think every member of every church would respect their church more if they knew the fight that had been staged with the devil to make their church what it is today".[1]

What a profound statement. Church history is indeed the story of how individual congregations have remained faithful to God amidst an ever-present spiritual conflict. At the fall of the Berlin Wall, German-Iranian artist Kani Alvai and French artist Muriel Raoux painted a mural with the words, "Many small people, who in many small places do many small things, can alter the face of the world." These words

---

[1]Jerome S. Robinson. *A Short History of The MT. Olive Baptist Church*. Drake Printers, Tuscaloosa. Al, 1959, iii.

have always stuck with me, especially when I remember the power everyday people deploy when they consistently take small steps toward a life-changing future.

In 1963, the Berlin Wall might not have fallen on Skyland Boulevard, but another significant event occurred—one which would shape and grow the Kingdom of God for generations in East Tuscaloosa. The story of this church does not begin with influential people and grand designs. Instead, the story of Skyland Boulevard Baptist is one of many small people who, in small ways, did many small things to grow the Kingdom of God.

STANDING ON THE
SHOULDERS OF GIANTS

TO JEROME AND JIMMY,

THANK YOU

CHAPTER ONE
THE MISSION

The best place to start in any story is the beginning. Skyland Boulevard Baptist Church's story began with the congregation of Calvary Baptist in Tuscaloosa, AL. Calvary Baptist was a growing and thriving church that developed a heart to plant churches within Tuscaloosa County. Calvary's heart for church planting resulted in the planting of Lakeview Baptist, South Highlands Baptist, Northridge Baptist, and Skyland Baptist.

In the early 1960s, Calvary purchased a lot on Hargrove Road, south of Skyland Boulevard, to establish a mission. However, as the plans for the mission developed, the church voted to exchange the Hargrove Road property, with member Eddie Gray Jones, for a parcel of property he owned on Skyland Boulevard. In February 1963, Rev. Jerome Robinson, a former Tuscaloosa County pastor who had recently joined Calvary, was asked to become the pastor of what was then called the "Highway 11 By-Pass Mission" at a salary of $100 per week.

Jerome Stancil Robinson

Jerome Stancil Robinson was born in Birmingham, Alabama on November 22nd, 1924. Jerome graduated from Brookwood High School in 1943, and after graduation, he quickly signed up to join the U.S. Army.

Jerome joined the Allied Army after D-day and participated in the Allied race to Berlin. Jerome fought in the Battle of the Bulge and the Battle of the Rhineland.[2] The Battle of the Bulge was the last great offensive by the German Army in WW II. The 5th and 6th Panzer Armies battered the American positions in the Ardennes Forrest for 3 months. Sitting in a foxhole under withering German fire, Jerome promised God that if he survived the battle, he would dedicate his life to serving Him. Many soldiers made similar promises but quickly recanted upon the Armistice. Jerome was different, and almost eight years after the guns fell silent on the Western Front, he was ready to pastor his first church.

---

[2]Melissa Connell, *The Tuscaloosa News: Saturday January 7th 1989.*

Jerome pastored two churches before coming to Skyland. Firstly, Mt. Olive Baptist Church in Tuscaloosa, AL, from 1953 – 1961. Secondly, Liberty Hill Baptist Church in Clanton, AL from 1961 – 1963.[3] During these years, Jerome attended the University of Alabama, graduating with a Bachelor of Science in 1961, a Master of Arts in 1963, and a Master of Science in 1965. Jerome was also an author, having written the history of Mt. Olive Baptist Church in 1959.

After leaving Liberty Hill, Jerome moved back to Tuscaloosa and started to attend Calvary Baptist Church. With Jerome on board, Calvary Baptist then voted to have the missions committee and the trustees secure a loan, not to exceed $28,000, to build the first unit of the mission. Calvary Baptist also requested that the Tuscaloosa County Baptist Association provide Calvary with a $2,500 interest-free loan from its mission fund. Two months later, Calvary borrowed $35,000 from the City National Bank of Tuscaloosa for the mission.[4]

---

[3] Jerome Stancil Robinson Profile: https://prabook.com/web/jerome_stancil.robinson/369887

[4] *The Rich Legacy of Calvary Baptist Church*, 129-130.

The First Service

The preparation was complete. What started as a dream became a reality. On June 2nd, 1963, the first service of Calvary Baptist Mission began with Sunday School at 1:15 pm and the Worship Service at 2 pm. The new congregation met under the slogan "A Growing Church for a Growing Community." Although the bulletins advertised an air-conditioned venue, this did not seem to be the case. It was 100 degrees that first Sunday and someone from the congregation groaned during the service that the air-conditioning wasn't working. Many years later, Jerome would write in the 10th-anniversary directory that it wasn't that the air conditioning wasn't working: it was. It was that there was no air conditioning in the first place.[5]

The first services were at the Seventh-Day Advent Church on Skyland Boulevard until the new building was ready. Jerome preached the first ever sermon for this Mission with the sermon title, "The Church, A

---

[5] *Skyland Baptist Directory: Church History*, 1973.

House of Prayer." The weekly offering was $121, and the Wednesday Prayer Meeting attendance was 19.

In his pastor's notes, Jerome challenged the congregation in two ways. First, invite someone to church the next week, and second, for more church members to join the softball team. Jerome wrote, "Calvary Mission has won their last two softball games. All interested men report for action. You are needed!"[6]

The first members of the church were:

Rev. Jerome Robinson (Pastor)

Mrs. Jerome Robinson

Miss Shelia Robinson

Deborah Robinson

Mr. James Gulledge

Mrs. James Gulledge

Mrs. John Thrasher

Mrs. Ruby Dean Gilliland

---

[6]Skyland Boulevard Bulletins, June 1963 - December 1965: Sunday June 9th 1963.

Mr. Jimmy Gilliland

Mr. Jim Wallace

Mrs. Jim Wallace

Mr. William Brown

Miss Mamie Mathews (Pianist)

By August 1963, the first unit of the building finished construction, and a name change quickly followed. On August 25th, 1963, Calvary Baptist Mission became Skyland Boulevard Baptist Mission. The membership voted on this name, which was already on the bulletins for the first-ever revival the following week. Jerome provided six ways to kill a revival which are still applicable today.

Six Ways to Kill a Revival[7]

1. Don't attend, but if you do, come late.
2. Find fault with everything and everybody
3. Leave all the visiting and praying to the preacher.
4. Don't invite anyone to the services.
5. Don't help with the singing.

---

[7]Ibid., Sunday, August 25th, 1963.

6. Just go through the revival, don't let it go through you.

The 30,000 Movement

Church planting was front and center of the Southern Baptist Convention in the Early 1960s due to the 30,000 Movement. The 30,000 Movement was an effort of Southern Baptist churches to establish 30,000 new churches and missions from 1956 – 1964. The program was part of the Baptist Jubilee Advance (1959 – 1964), designed to celebrate the 150th anniversary of the organization of Baptist work in America. The stated purpose of the movement was "to establish 10,000 churches and 20,000 missions by 1964 to reach, teach, and win individuals to Christ and train them to live Christian lives." The program's slogan was "Every Church with a Mission."[8]

An influential leader of the 30,000 Movement was Arkansas pastor Dr. W.O. Vought. Dr. Vought provided five metrics to help Missions understand

---

[8]*Southern Baptist Historical Library & Archives*: 30,000 Movement Collection AR 686. https://sbhla.org/finding_aids/30000-movement/.

when they had grown healthy enough to leave the care of the mother church. The TCBA used these metrics and applied them to the Skyland Mission.

The five metrics were that a mission should be mothered until 1) it had trained leadership for an effective organization. 2) it had enough income to support itself – all missions included. 3) it had an adequate building, equipment, and program; 4) all the greenwood had seasoned out; 5) it had a full-time pastor.[9] Under the watch care of Calvary Baptist and the TCBA, it would take over four years to achieve these five metrics for Skyland Baptist Mission.

The TCBA semi-annual meeting on October 9th, 1967, was momentous. In this meeting, Skyland finally graduated from a mission to an independent church. Carol Hatchel, the TCBA Director of Mission wrote,

"The fall semi-annual session convened Monday afternoon, October 9th, 1967, at the West End Church. Mr. John Christy directed the congregation in singing "I AM Thine, O Lord" and "Tell the Story of Jesus." Rev. Hollis Hendon, moderator and host pastor welcomed

---

[9] Carol T. Hatchel. *History of the Tuscaloosa County Baptist Association: Two Decades and More 1953-1974*: Weatherford Publishing Company, 1989, 61.

the messengers causing all to feel the warmth of Christian fellowship. Then Rev. Jack Mayfield, pastor of Grants Creek, was presented to give the devotion. Skyland Blvd Baptist Church was welcomed into the Association with great joy. Skyland became a self-supporting independent church with 194 members, 224 enrolled in Sunday School and 133 in Church training."[10]

As we draw to the end of the first chapter, let's remember Winston Churchill's words in 1942. As WW 11 changed course Churchill explained, "This is not the end. It is not even the beginning of the end. But perhaps, the end of the beginning" Many years later, the Tuscaloosa Churchill, Nick Saban, would say something similar upon winning the 2010 National Championship. "This is not the end. It is the beginning." Both these sentiments echo the energy of Skyland Baptist Church in 1967. The foundation was prepared, and there awaited an exciting future.

---

[10]*Homecoming Celebration 50th Anniversary*: History of Skyland.

A military photo of Jerome Robinson

Jerome Robinson in the Tuscaloosa News

Skyland Baptists Plan To Use New Building

Members of the Skyland Boulevard Baptist Mission will move into their new church tomorrow, when a series of revival services will begin.

Revival services will be held Sunday through Sept. 1 at 7:30 daily with the pastor, Rev. Jerome Robinson, as evangelist and Dick Barrett of Calvary Baptist Church as chorister.

The mission at 3320 Skyland Boulevard, just west of Hargrove Road, is a two-story concrete block and brick veneer structure. It has about 6,000 square feet of floor space and a sanctuary capable of seating approximately 300 persons.

The building is centrally air conditioned and heated with five classrooms and other necessary facilities.

Regular Sunday services of the mission, organized by Calvary Baptist Church, include church school at 9:50 a.m., worship service at 11 a.m. and 7:30 p.m. and Training Union at 6:30 p.m.

Members of the congregation have been meeting in the nearby Seventh Day Adventist Church since the mission was formed earlier this year.

Clippings from the Tuscaloosa News about the launch of the Skyland Mission

ANNOUNCING
OUR
SERVICES

Dear Friend:

The Calvary Baptist Mission which is located on the US II Bypass will move into their new building Sunday, August 25th. This Mission will be called the Skyland Boulevard Baptist Mission until the Mission is constituted into a Church, and then it will be known as the Skyland Boulevard Baptist Church.

We are hoping that you can worship with us in our new building Sunday morning. Our goal in Sunday school is 150. We hope that you will help us reach our goal.

Our revival begins Sunday morning, August 25th and will continue through Sunday, August 31. Our services will begin each night at 7:30. The music will be under the direction of Dick Barrett, minister of music at the Calvary Baptist Church of Tuscaloosa. The evangelist will be the pastor.

Yours In Christ

Jerome Robinson

Jerome Robinson, Pastor

PS. Please look for our special announcement in the Tuscaloosa News Saturday, August 24th.

A 1963 invitation to the Skyland Boulevard Baptist Mission

CALVARY BAPTIST MISSION

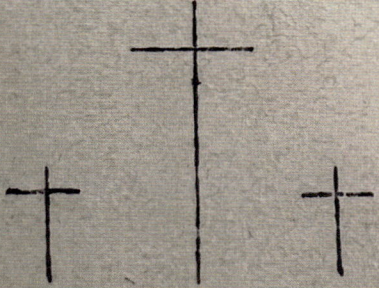

WELCOME

"A Growing Church In A Growing Community"

(Air-Conditioned For Your Comfort)

First bulletin as Calvary Baptist Mission

Founding Membership, 1963

SKYLAND BOULEVARD BAPTIST MISSION

(3320 East Skyland Boulevard)

†   †   †

WELCOME!!!

"A Growing Church In A Growing Community"

†   †   †

(Air Conditioned For Your Comfort)

First bulletin as Skyland Boulevard Baptist Mission

SKYLAND

BOULEVARD

BAPTIST CHURCH

WELCOME

First bulletin as Skyland Boulevard Baptist Church

CHAPTER TWO
TO GOD BE THE GLORY

"There's also no doubt that we could be doing twice what we are if all members would bow to their knees and ask God's will for their lives and put it into practice here at Skyland. I believe and know that the future for Skyland Boulevard Baptist Church is great. God is going to build a great Church here at 3320 Skyland Boulevard."

Bro. Jerome Robinson

Shortly before the tenth anniversary, Skyland received its first national accolade. The church was recognized by *Church Training* magazine in February 1972, after considerable searching through other Baptist periodicals as the only Baptist church in the Southern Baptist Convention to have 100% of their membership in church training. The magazine cited the enthusiasm of the new members as the leading factor for this achievement.[11]

Skyland also led the way within the TCBA with the lowest resident non-membership, the percentage of Church members in Sunday School, and the average dollar per member received through the church. In light of this news, Jerome rallied the congregation and declared, "today, and in the future, our tongues shall praise Him and say, 'TO GOD BE THE GLORY'."[12]

Sanctuary Renovation

The 70s and 80s saw remarkable growth and expansion in people and facilities. The church added an education unit in 1974 for $109,000.00. This unit included a fellowship hall, a nursery department downstairs, and another restroom. Upstairs housed six Sunday School rooms. This renovation eliminated

---

[11]Skyland Baptist Directory: Church History, 1973.

[12]Ibid.

the three temporary Sunday School rooms in the Sanctuary and created more seating capacity.

Another facility upgrade occurred in 1980 and 1982. In 1980, the Sanctuary remodel included a balcony addition for $125,000.00. On November 9th, 1980, at 10 am, the church observed a unique dedication service. The choir opened and closed the dedication service with the hymn "To God be the Glory."

An invocation was given by Gil Sentell, who served as the building committee chairman (Gil is still a deacon at Skyland and a faithful Sunday School teacher). Jerome led the recognition of the visiting workers who carried out the renovation. Jerome closed with a responsive reading. The congregation stood together, held hands, and proclaimed,

> "To the Eternal God our Father, maker of heaven and earth. Author and giver of life, who in the person of Jesus Christ his Son has made known to us the patience and power of his redeeming love, and who by his gracious Spirit is ever seeking to bring light into our darkness,
>
> **We dedicate this church**

To the preaching of the Gospel of Christ, and to our belief that the principles of his Gospel will bring light, healing, and peace to mankind,

We dedicate this church

For the training of Youth and the building of Character, for the giving of hope and courage to all human hearts, and for the teaching of morality, justice, and righteousness,

We dedicate this church

For comfort to those who mourn, for strength to those who are tempted, for help in right living, for the welfare of the home, for the guidance of youth, for the salvation of all the people

We dedicate this church

For the furtherance of the worldwide program of Jesus, for the encouragement of missionary endeavor at home and abroad for Christian education,

We dedicate this church

For the promotion of Christian unity which sees beneath all formal differences a bond of fellowship and endeavors to keep the unity of the Spirit in the bond of peace,

We dedicate this church

That this may be for all people a House of Prayer, that men may be conscious that God is in this place, that it may be to them none other than the House of God and the Gate of Heaven,

We dedicate this church

The God of peace, who brought again from the dead our Lord Jesus, that great Shepherd of the sheep, through the blood of the everlasting covenant, make us perfect in every good work to do his will, working in us that which is well-pleasing in his sight, through Jesus Christ; to whom be glory forever and ever. Amen."

Looking back, these words are very poignant. As the old saying goes, "the proof of the pudding is in the eating." Today, it is over 40 years since this dedication. I am thankful the congregation did not simply say these words but acted upon them. May we join hands with those who have gone before us and renew this dedication today.

Needing more facilities for the growing youth department, the Christian Life Center, now Family Life Center, was built in 1982. This addition to the facilities included seven Sunday School rooms, a gym, a kitchen, restrooms, and a storage area.[13] A company from Colombus, MS, built the shell of the metal butler building. The men of the church primarily completed the rest of the work.

Jim Grubbs' brother worked in South Alabama laying tile, and he came to Skyland and laid the indoor tile for the Basketball court. The remaining rooms and kitchen were built by the men of the church who met together on Saturdays. Men such as Gil Sentell, Jerry Mims, Jim Grubbs, Edwin Lawrence, worked faithfully to complete the work.

Worship Leadership

Skyland has a rich tradition of Godly men and women leading worship. Below is a list of every worship leader from the days of Calvary Baptist Mission to the present day. Upon reading the list, I think you would join me in making a special note of thanks to Levert Lawrence.

---

[13] Homecoming Celebration 50th Anniversary: History of Skyland.

Levert holds the record of serving as the Worship Leader on five different occasions for a total of nine years. It is lay leadership like Levert's, which is the hallmark of the early years of Skyland. Upon Levert's decision to step down as worship leader, Jerome wrote, "It is with deep regret that we enjoy your beautiful music for the last time today. We wish God's best for you and the family. Skyland has been known under your direction as a church of beautiful music. We thank you, Levert, Patsy, Russell, and David".[14] Below is a list of all worship leaders at Skyland.

Choir Directors 1963 - 2023[15]

Edith Stallworth: 1963-65

George Bennett: 1966-69

Dr. Gaston Calvert: 1960 - 1970

Benny Russell: 1970-1971

Gene Hobson: 1971-72

---

[14]*Skyland Boulevard Bulletins*, Jan 1974 – Dec 1975: June 30th 1974.

[15]Homecoming Celebration 50th Anniversary: History of Skyland.

Doris Haley: 1972-72

Levert Lawrence: 1972-74

Frank Deaver: 1974-74

Lavert Lawrence: 1974-76

Wright Ingram: 1976-77

Levert Lawrence:1977-78

Scott Stokes: 1978-82

Lavert Lawrence: 1982-83

Gaines Hyche: 1983

Levert Lawrence: 1983-1986

Carl Walker: 1987

Bryan Skinner: 1987-1998

Jim Young: 1998-2017

Josh Hill: 2017- Present

Revival

The theme of revival is woven through the history of Skyland. Traditionally, revival is a focused time of prayer, worship, preaching, and fellowship. Through revival, the members of Skyland, individually and corporately, have experienced the Holy Spirit move in incredible ways.

The revival of 1987 holds a special place in the heart of our church. In July 1987, Skyland held a lay revival as Jerome was in the Philippines leading a crusade. As Jerome was out of the country, laymen conducted the revival entirely. The revival began with the preaching of Scott Souls on the parable of the Wheat and the Tares, and laymen in the church, such as Jack Ezell, led other nights.

The singular focus of the 1987 Revival was seeking the Holy Spirit to work in the lives of church members. Looking back, we can see this is precisely what happened. Over 40 people gave their lives to Jesus, and many others rededicated their lives. Many of these members are still worshiping at the church to this day. Carl and Margarite Walker sang "Breathe on Me" as special music on the Sunday morning, urging the Holy Spirit to come and work as revival began.

As Scott Sauls led the invitation, Carl and Margarite's daughter, Frances James, left the organ she was playing and came forward to give her life to Jesus. What a wonderful picture of God working through the families of Skyland and our larger faith family. As we end this chapter, let us meditate on the words of the old hymn Carl and Margarite Walker sang all those years ago. Please pray for God to work like this again in Skyland Baptist Church.

Breathe on me, Breath of God,
fill me with life anew,
that I may love the way you love,
and do what you would do.

Breathe on me, Breath of God,
until my heart is pure,
until my will is one with yours,
to do and to endure.

Breathe on me, Breath of God,
so shall I never die,
but live with you the perfect life
for all eternity.

The First Retirement

It's a testament to the shepherd and the sheep that it was 26 years before Skyland witnessed its first pastoral retirement. Jerome was getting older and unable to complete the ministry he had once performed. Jerome clarified, "I'm retiring, but I'm not resigning. I didn't retire to go to another church. I retired because of my health. I'm one of those hyperactive people, and I knew that if I couldn't do what I wanted to do, I didn't want to make a flop trying".[16]

Jerome traveled extensively with many trips to the Philippines. From 1984-1986 Jerome served as a Trustee of the Foreign Mission Board (now the I.M.B) and helped to plant ten churches throughout the Philippine Islands with the Gene Williams Evangelistic Association. Jerome traveled around the world twice, visiting the Holy Land in 1970, including visits to Korea.[17]

As Jerome got older, the effects of travel took their toll. Jerome was diagnosed with liver cirrhosis,

---

[16]Melissa Connell, *The Tuscaloosa News: Saturday January 7th 1989.*

[17]Ibid.

which he believed he developed on one of his trips to the Philippines. On top of liver cirrhosis, Jerome survived three heart attacks, making shepherding harder and harder.

Jerome wished to use his retirement to travel again to the Philippines and write another book. Jerome had already written three books, including The Separation of Church and State and its Effect on Church and State (if anyone can find a copy of this book, please let me know). Throughout his life, Jerome received three degrees from the University of Alabama and, in 1985, his Doctor of Ministry Degree from Luther Rice Seminary.[18]

With the announcement of Jerome's retirement, Skyland moved its attention toward finding a new pastor for the first time. When Jerome first learned about this potential church plant, it was called Highway 11 Bypass Mission and now it was an established healthy church reaching East Tuscaloosa with the Gospel.

When I think of Jerome's faithfulness, I am reminded of Theodore Roosevelt's "Citizenship in a Republic" speech. In this speech, Roosevelt shared the

---

[18]Confirmed with Luther Rice on April 25th 2023.

importance of being the Man in the Arena. It's easy to criticize as a spectator but much harder to roll up your sleeves and get the job done. When it comes to church planting, many people critique what church planters do without ever getting their hands dirty. I am thankful that from 1963 – 1989 Jerome was the Man in the Arena. Roosevelt described,

> "It is not the critic who counts; not the man who points out how the strong man stumbles, or where the doer of deeds could have done them better. The credit belongs to the man who is actually in the arena, whose face is marred by dust and sweat and blood; who strives valiantly; who errs, who comes short again and again, because there is no effort without error and shortcoming; but who does actually strive to do the deeds; who knows great enthusiasms, the great devotions; who spends himself in a worthy cause; who at the best knows in the end the triumph of high achievement, and who at the worst, if he fails, at least fails while daring greatly, so that his place shall never be with those cold

and timid souls who neither know victory nor defeat."[19]

Theodore Roosevelt, April 23[rd,] 1910.

---

[19]https://www.theodorerooseveltcenter.org/Lear
n-About-TR/TR-Encyclopedia/Culture-and-Society/Man-
in-the-Arena.aspx

SKYLAND BOULEVARD

BAPTIST

CHURCH

TUSCALOOSA   **ALABAMA**

DIRECTORY 1982
JEROME S. ROBINSON, PASTOR

1982 Church Directory

Skyland Baptist Chapel, 1981

1st Row (L-R): Bill Burroughs, Gil Sentell, Larry Williams, Joe Barton, Jerry Mims, Aubrey Noland. 2nd Row; Dennis Crocker, Jack Ezell, Ed Barnette, Gary Hamner, Mike Harris, Gene Kirk and Jim Grubbs, (Not Pictured) Carl Walker, Noel Brock, Harold Oliver and Roscoe Morrison.

Deacons, 1982

Pastor Jerome, 1982

Jerome and Lila Robinson, 1992

Saturday, January 7, 1989 THE TUSCALOOSA NEWS

Skyland Boulevard Baptist losing pastor of 25 years

By MELISSA CONNELL
News Intern

The Rev. Jerome Robinson

Crouching in a foxhole during World War II, the Rev. Jerome Robinson made a promise to devote his life to God if he made it out of the war alive.

Other soldiers made similar promises, often broken when the last shots were fired. But Robinson kept his word and even began a new church, Skyland Boulevard Baptist, less than 20 years after his discharge from the Army.

Now, 35 years into Robinson's preaching career, he has decided to step down from the pulpit because of health problems. But though many of the burdens of pastoring will be lifted, Robinson said he still plans to preach.

"I'll probably be able to preach every Sunday," he said, since more than 15 Baptist churches in Tuscaloosa are now without a permanent pastor.

"I'm retiring, but I'm not resigning. I didn't retire to go to another church. I retired because of my health. I'm one of those hyperactive people, and I knew that if I couldn't do what I wanted to do, I didn't want to make a flop out trying."

Robinson said he is no longer able to knock on a thousand doors each year, or get up in the morning hours to go see someone in the hospital.

As pastor, Robinson said he went to the hospitals almost every day, and visited other ailing church members at home or in nursing homes. In fact, he still makes several visits each week.

"But that's what the Lord challenged his ministers to do in the Bible," Robinson said. "To look after the fatherless, the widows and the poor."

And now, Robinson must look after himself.

In the past 12 years, he has had three heart attacks, resulting in open-heart surgery. And though Robinson said he has never smoked one cigarette or drunk any alcohol, he also suffers from cirrhosis of the liver.

Robinson said he believes he developed the disease on one of his trips to the Philippine Islands, where he has evangelized for several months during the past five or six years.

From 1984 until 1986, Robinson served as a member of the Foreign Mission Board and helped established 10 churches on the islands with the assistance of the Gene Williams Evangelistic Association.

Robinson said he has traveled around the world twice, beginning with a trip to the Holy Land in 1976 and including visits to Korea.

But though Robinson has traveled extensively, he said most of his time has been spent at the 600-member Skyland Boulevard Baptist Church, where he has been pastor for 25 years.

Ever since found religious salvation at age 8, Robinson said he thought he might become a preacher one day.

"It was on my mind," he said. "As I grew older, it became clearer. But as a kid, I just thought about it. There was always that thought in the back of my mind.

"When I was young, I picked out the preachers I liked. By that, I mean their style," he said.

"I don't like it for a preacher to get too loud and too wild like I've seen some preachers do. But I don't want to listen to someone read their sermon in a monotone, either.

"The way I've judged my own self is that I've discovered people will come back and listen to you if they think you believe in what you're saying," Robinson said.

He compares preachers to radio sportscasters.

"Like when a man calls a football game, if they're talking in a monotone, people will look for another station," said Robinson.

Recently, the preacher was the recipient of many honors. On his 64th birthday, Nov. 22, 1988, a flag was flown over the Capitol in Washington, D.C., in Robinson's honor, and Tuscaloosa Mayor Al DuPont proclaimed the day Jerome Robinson Day. However, festivities were interrupted by the aftermath of the tornado that ripped through Southwood just two days earlier.

Robinson is a candidate for Baptist Minister of the Year in Tuscaloosa.

During his time away from the pulpit, Robinson has much he wants to accomplish. First, he said he would like to read at least one book each week.

"And I want to go back to the Philippines at least one more time," Robinson said. "I'd like to do a little writing maybe. I don't know whether I will, but I'd like to write at least one more book."

Robinson has written three books, including "The Separation of Church and State and Its Effect on Church and State."

After graduation from Brookwood High School in 1943, Robinson served in the Army, fighting in the Battle of the Bulge and the Battle of the Rhineland during World War II.

Two years later, he was wounded in Belgium. He received not only an honorable discharge but also the Purple Heart, the World War II Victory Medal, the Good Conduct Medal, three bronze stars, the American Theatre Service Ribbon and the EAME Theatre Service Ribbon.

After he returned from service, he married his wife, Lila, and now has two daughters and four grandchildren.

Robinson later received three degrees from the University of Alabama and a doctor's degree from Luther Rice Seminary.

Pastor Jerome retirement writeup, 1989

Skyland Boulevard Baptist Church

3320 East Skyland Boulevard

Tuscaloosa, Alabama 35401

Telephone 553-7412

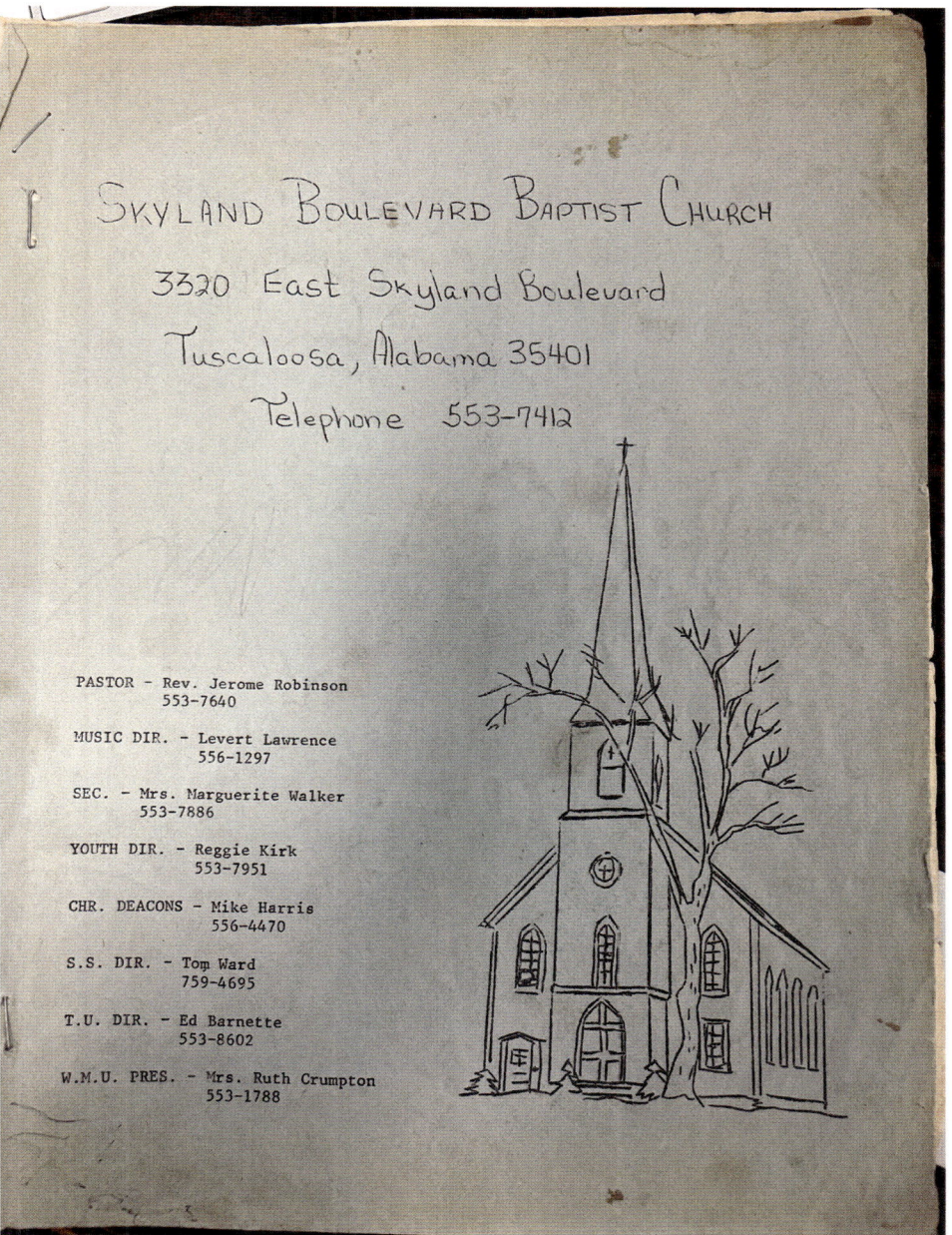

PASTOR - Rev. Jerome Robinson
       553-7640

MUSIC DIR. - Levert Lawrence
       556-1297

SEC. - Mrs. Marguerite Walker
       553-7886

YOUTH DIR. - Reggie Kirk
       553-7951

CHR. DEACONS - Mike Harris
       556-4470

S.S. DIR. - Tom Ward
       759-4695

T.U. DIR. - Ed Barnette
       553-8602

W.M.U. PRES. - Mrs. Ruth Crumpton
       553-1788

1978 Church Directory

Bryan Skinner, Music Minister

Front of Church, 1982

CHAPTER THREE
WE'RE GONNA WIN

I thank my God always when I remember you in my
prayers, because I hear of your love and of the faith
that you have toward the Lord Jesus and for all the
saints, and I pray that the sharing of your faith may
become effective for the full knowledge of every good
thing that is in us for the sake of Christ. For I have
derived much joy and comfort from your love, my
brother, because the hearts of the saints have been
refreshed through you.

I love you in the Lord![20]

Jimmy Garner, 2008

Jimmy's Early Years

Jimmy Garner was born on April 5th 1939, in
Fackler, AL. He is the Son of Walter and Mildred
Garner and graduated from Jackson County High

---

[20] Pastor's Notes. 2008 Church Directory.

School. Jimmy married Carolyn on August 16, 1958. Together they would have one daughter, Paulette. Jimmy wrote, "At about the age of twelve, I attended a VBS at Friendship Baptist Church of Fackler, Alabama. During the response time, my best friend who was about five years older went forward to accept Christ and I went forward because he did. I filled out a little white card and was dunked in the water and placed on the church roll but I was not saved. My letter remained at Friendship Baptist Church until I accepted Christ".[21]

Jimmy worked for Jim Walter Homes and attended Woodville Baptist Church with his family. It was not until January 5th 1975 that Jimmy came forward during the invitation and gave his life to Jesus.

Almost two years later Jimmy felt the Lord call him to pastoral ministry in December 1977. Jimmy was the top salesman two years running at Jim Walter Homes in all of their 38 States. However, the stress was crippling. Jimmy didn't have peace and believed the Lord was calling him to Pastoral ministry.

---

[21]Jimmy Garner, Biographical Note. Kept in Church Office.

The weekend before Christmas in 1977 had significant effect in the course of Jimmy's life. On Friday, December 16th, 1977, Jimmy came home from work and told Carolyn he was under tremendous pressure and he believed the Lord was calling him to leave Jim Walter. Jimmy had a key to the church and he went that same night and prayed for the Lord's leading. Alone at the altar of Woodville Baptist on a cold dark December night Jimmy told God "I'm giving you everything I have. My family, career, and possessions take them and use them". Jimmy told me, "You are never more at peace than when you give everything you have to the Lord".

Jimmy had peace in the Lord's calling. The next day on Saturday December 17th Jimmy went to his work office and cleared his desk. On Sunday December 18th Jimmy attended the local brotherhood breakfast hosted at his church. He told the assembled men he had surrendered to the call to preach and was resigning from Jim Walter Homes the next day.

A few of the men tried to talk him out of it. Reminding him he only had two years until he could claim his retirement and all the benefits from the company. Jimmy's nickname was "Nervy" because he had the nerve to do anything. And true to his name

Nervy wouldn't back down. He was giving everything to the Lord.

Howard Johnson the pastor of Faith Baptist Church in Scottsboro, AL was present at the breakfast and invited Jimmy to preach at his church the following Sunday night. Jimmy accepted the invitation. The next day on Monday December 19th 1977 Jimmy called his boss in Huntsville and resigned from Jim Walter Homes. Jimmy returned home and began writing his first sermon which he preached on Christmas Night 1977.

Woodville Baptist ordained Jimmy on January 29, 1978 and three days later, on February 1st 1978, Jimmy started as the pastor of Bethany Baptist Church in Section Alabama. Jimmy had only preached four sermons before becoming pastor. Jimmy documented, "I preached my first message on Christmas night at Faith Baptist Church in Scottsboro, Alabama; my second message on New Year's Eve night at Shiloh Baptist Church of Scottsboro, Alabama; my third message on New Year's Day at Bethany Baptist Church of Section, Alabama; and my fourth message New Year's night at Bethany Baptist Church. I preached my fifth message, as a pastor, at Bethany Baptist Church on the first Sunday in February 1978. God honors faith!"[22]

The journey of Jimmy's faith did not end when Jimmy became a pastor. It was only the beginning. Jimmy added, "Very soon my faith was challenged. I had been pastoring, my first church, Bethany Baptist, for about six months. My wife, Carolyn, developed a lump in her breast. I was walking down the hall of the hospital toward her room and the doctor stopped me and told me that it was cancer and her breast had to go. I walked into the room and she was crying. I asked her to recall that I had given her and everything I had to the Lord and I was going to serve Him at all cost. Her dad was not saved and he was a member of the Masonic Lodge. He had told me if a person would do the things they did they would be all right. I got Carolyn by the hand and told her we were going to pray a hard prayer, "Whatever it takes to save her dad." I never asked God to heal my wife. I prayed for God to save her Dad regardless. The next Sunday night he came to church at Bethany Baptist but never accepted Christ. The next Sunday he went to church with his wife. A converted Jew by the name of Rocky Freeman

---

[22]Jimmy Garner, Biographical Note. Kept in Church Office.

was preaching and he was saved. I baptized my father-in-law two weeks later into the fellowship of First Baptist Church of Stevenson, Alabama. God honors faith! When a person surrenders all to Jesus Christ their faith will be challenged".[23]

Over the next ten years, Jimmy would pastor at:

- Bethany Baptist, Section AL (February 1st 1978 – February 1st 1980)
- Hollywood Baptist, Hollywood AL (February 1st 1980 – December 5th 1982)
- Open Acres Baptist, Montgomery, AL (December 6th 1982 – October 1st 1986).
- FBC Louisville, Louisville, MS (October 10th 1986 – July 30th 1989) - Associate Pastor.

Jimmy Arrives at Skyland

In the fall of 1988, Jimmy Garner was preaching revival services at Rosedale Baptist in Tuscaloosa. A visitor informed about Jerome's retirement and asked

---

[23] Jimmy Garner, Biographical Note. Kept in Church Office.

him to submit a resume. At the time Jimmy was serving as the Pastor of Education and Evangelism at FBC Louisville, MS.

Jimmy submitted a resume and was soon invited to Tuscaloosa to meet the congregation. Jimmy agreed on the condition he stayed for the whole weekend. Jimmy fellowshipped with the church on the Friday night, answered questions from the congregation in the fellowship hall on Saturday night, and preached on Sunday morning. As Jimmy preached, he shared slides on the Over Head Projector of how Sunday School would be his primary strategy for growth.

The congregation enjoyed Jimmy's preaching and his passion for evangelism. Skyland officially asked Jimmy to be their pastor and he accepted starting in August, 1989. When Jimmy arrived, Reggie Kirk was the Associate Pastor and Bryan Skinner was the Minister of Music. Jerome still attended the church and bestowed the title of Pastor Emeritus. Occasionally, Jerome preached at other churches and enjoyed a brief stint as the interim pastor at Hargrove Road Baptist Church.

Jimmy's Team

Bryan Skinner came to Skyland in 1987, part-time, as the Minister of Music. Bryan worked full-time at Bell South while juggling responsibilities at Skyland. Bryan served in the twilight of Jerome's pastorate and helped transition to Jimmy. Bryan primarily led the choir, music ministries, and the youth group as needed. Bryan developed and led the youth choir on many trips across the Southeast.

I called Bryan to ask him about his memories of Skyland and enjoyed a great conversation. Bryan still leads and ministers to people as the Worship Pastor at Brainerd Baptist Church in Chattanooga, TN. On the day I spoke with him Bryan he was just leaving the hospital after visiting one of his choir members. Bryan shared how much he loved the Skyland congregation and how they cared for his family.

Bryan reminisced on the bond between the staff. Speaking fondly of how they enjoyed activities together as friends. Bryan first felt called to full-time ministry when he was 16 years old, but it was the encouragement of Jimmy to attend seminary which led Bryan to consider this calling again. After much prayer and deliberation, Bryan and his family left Skyland in June of 1998 to attend New Orleans Baptist

Theological Seminary. After serving in different churches throughout the Southeast, Bryan currently serves at Brainerd Baptist.

In 1991 Jimmy invited his friend John Merk from Mississippi to lead Revival at Skyland. Reggie Kirk had recently left to become a pastor and Jimmy and Bryan Skinner were left to hold down the fort. Merk noticed the strain Jimmy was under and told Jimmy he needed help. Merk recommended a man he met during revival services in Louisiana. Merk explained, "you need help Jimmy, you need Sal".

Sal Barone was serving at Memorial Baptist Church in Bogalusa, LA, and met John Merk during a revival service in the State. In light of this recommendation, Jimmy called together the Long-Range Planning Committee. They travelled to Talladega for the night to pray and seek God's wisdom. The team left Talladega with the sense God was leading them to approach Sal. The problem is Jimmy had never met Sal. Jimmy drove to Bogalusa and told Sal God had led him to offer Sal a position at Skyland.

In 1991 Sal, his wife Claudia, and children Josh, Jennifer, and Hannah moved to Tuscaloosa and began their ministry at Skyland. Sal served as the Minister of Education and Singles from 1991 to 1997.

Sal enjoyed his singles ministry and believed through his time at Skyland, "God taught him how to lead like Jesus".

One day Sal was singing to the residents at Clara Verner Towers, a nursing home close to the UA campus, when he felt the Lord convict and give him a heart for Senior Adult ministry. In 1981 Sal met Don Wilton in revival at FBC Chalmette, and this encounter would have seismic ramifications for the future of Skyland and Sal. In 1997 Don called Sal and asked him to join the pastoral staff at FBC Spartanburg, SC. After six months of careful deliberation, Sal, Claudia and the children left Skyland for South Carolina, where Sal would lead a successful ministry to Seniors Adults.

When I called Sal to ask him a few questions, he was in his office in Spartanburg. It was a joy to talk with a man I hardly knew, whose life has been transformed by Skyland's congregation. We both shared that through this loving congregation, we were being developed to be the leaders God has called us to be.

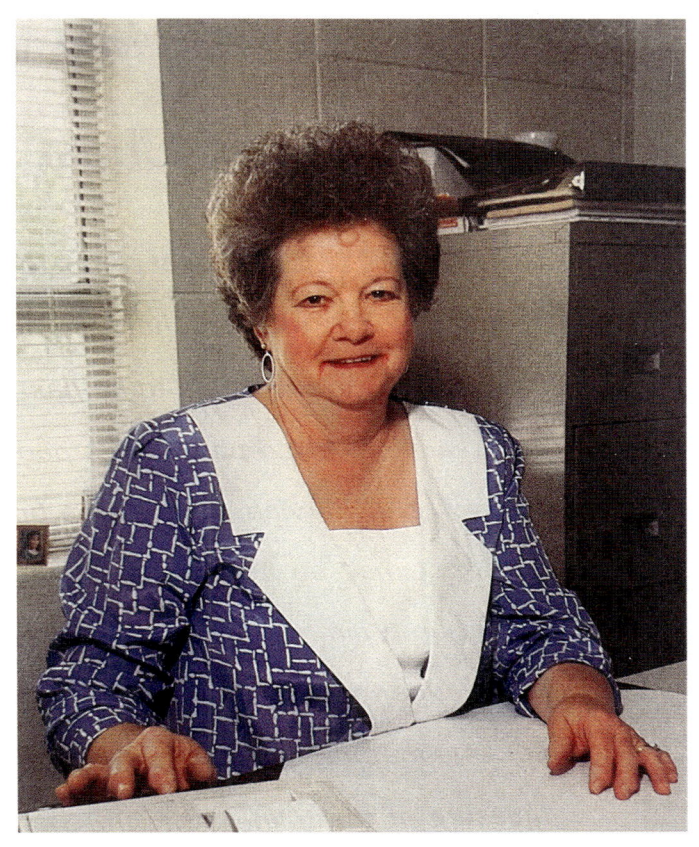

Marguerite Walker, Office Manager

Pastor Jimmy Garner, 1992

Jerome as Pastor Emeritus

Sal Barone as Associate Pastor

Pastor Jimmy Garner preaching, 1992

*Bryan Skinner, Minister of Music,
leading worship service 1992*

CHAPTER FOUR

A JIMMY, A JIM, AND A JON

"God has truly blessed Skyland Boulevard Baptist Church by giving us a loving congregation that loves the Lord and the local church. . . My ambition is to preach the Word of God in its entirety and lead the membership to love the Lord with all your heart and love, and serve each other with the love of Christ. . . I wish to thank Skyland Boulevard Baptist Church for the love you have shown to me, my family, and the staff of the church. This church has exhibited its love by having only two pastors in 50 years."[24]

Jimmy Garner 2015

Jim Young

Pastoral ministry can be challenging. One factor which makes it more enjoyable is working with great people. Jimmy was looking for another pastor to join

---

[24]Skyland Baptist Directory: Pastor's Notes, 2015.

the church after the departure of Sal Barone and Bryan Skinner. During this time, Jimmy reached out to an old friend in Mississippi who he knew through his work with Sunday school. His name was Jim Young.

Jim Young was serving as the Associate Pastor and Minister of Music at Calvary Baptist Church in West Point, Mississippi. Jimmy previously visited West Point and consulted on how to grow a thriving Sunday School ministry. Jim remembered how Jimmy's advice brought success to the church, and this meeting began a long friendship.

Often, when Jimmy traveled to Mississippi, he called Jim, and they would meet for lunch. Jim was struck by Jimmy's heart for evangelism. He described that whenever they were together, Jimmy shared the Gospel with whoever he met.

Jim respected Jimmy. When Jimmy invited him to apply for the open position at Skyland Jim embraced the opportunity. After much prayer and a visit to Tuscaloosa, Jim and his wife Fran felt they were called to come and serve at Skyland.

Jim Young was hired in 1998 as the Associate Pastor and Minister of Education. Due to Bryan Skinner leaving to pursue Seminary education, Jim offered to temporarily lead the worship ministry. Little did anyone know, but the interim turned out to be 19 years. Jim served faithfully as Education & Music Minister for all those years being an ever-present help to the congregation and to Jimmy.

It is a testament to Jim's servant heart that he led a ministry he was not hired to lead for 19 years without an ounce of grumbling. Like me, I'm sure you all had times when Jim was there for support and encouragement. I was blessed to serve with Jim for my first year at Skyland. In 2016, I started as the Student Pastor and I was grateful to have Jim's support and guidance in developing my ministry. Jim showed me what it looked like to love God and to love others. Thank you, Jim.

The Death of Jerome

Jerome died on January 26th 2001 at the VA Medical Center and was buried at Heritage Chapel in Tuscaloosa. Jimmy preached the funeral with many past and present deacons as pallbearers. I am encouraged that Jerome asked Jimmy to preach his funeral. It showed to me the love and respect that they had for each other.

Jimmy told me he regularly thanked Jerome from the pulpit for his service to Skyland. The only people who can truly understand the joys and trials of pastoring a church are the other men who have pastored that church previously or subsequently. Below is a copy of the obituary from The Tuscaloosa News on January 27th 2001.

TUSCALOOSA - Jerome Stancil Robinson, 76, died Jan. 26, 2001, at VA Medical Center. Services will be held at Heritage Chapel Funeral Home on Monday at 11 a.m. with Jimmy Garner officiating. Burial will be at Tuscaloosa Memorial Park. Visitation is tonight from 6 to 8 p.m. Heritage Chapel Funeral Home is directing.

He is survived by his wife, Lila Mae Robinson of Tuscaloosa; daughters, Sheila D. Harris of Marietta, Ga. and Deborah B. Barnette of Birmingham; grandchildren, Brian J. Harris, Stephanie B. O'Guinn, Tanya B. Stignani and Jason E. Barnette; great-grandchildren, Presley A. Stignani and Connor B. O'Guinn.

Mr. Robinson was a paratrooper during World War II. He was wounded during the Battle of the Bulge. He received the Bronze Star, Purple Heart and WWII Victory Medal. He also served as a machine gunner and was awarded the American Theatre Service Ribbon with bronze clusters. He graduated from the University of Alabama and from the New Orleans Baptist Theological Seminary. He ministered at Mt. Olive and Liberty Hill. The majority of his ministry was at Skyland Baptist Church for 25 years.

Pallbearers will be Ollie James Harris Jr., Edward C. Barnette Jr., Gary M. Stignani, Brian J. Harris, Jason E. Barnette, Noel Brock, Jack Ezell and Gil Sentell.

Honorary pallbearers are the present and past deacons of Skyland Baptist Church.[25]

Jon Wiggins

Jonathan David Wiggins was born June 4th 1982, in Birmingham, AL. Jon spent his early years in Tuscaloosa before moving to Haleyville, AL. In 1996 Jon moved back to Tuscaloosa graduating from Tuscaloosa Academy in 2000. Jon enrolled in Shelton State Community College before transferring to the

---

[25]Jerome Stancil Robinson Obituary, The Tuscaloosa News, January 27th 2001. https://www.tuscaloosanews.com/story/news/2001/01/28/jerome-stancil-robinson/27803579007/

University of Mobile and graduating with a Bachelor of Science in Christian Studies in 2004.

As Jon studied at Shelton State in 2001 and during the summers of 2002 and 2003 Jon served as the Youth Director at Eastern Hills Baptist Church in Tuscaloosa, AL. This opportunity to serve the church and his studies at Mobile gave Jon a pastor's heart for the church, particularly a heart for student ministry.

In the Tuscaloosa church world Pastors Jimmy Garner, Ken Cheek, and Herb Thomas are nicknamed the Trinity as they are always together. When Josh Howell left Skyland, there was a new Minister of Students vacancy. Jon's home church was Circlewood Baptist in Tuscaloosa and its pastor Herb Thomas, recommended Jon to Jimmy.

Jimmy listened to Herb and invited Jon to lunch to discuss Student Ministry. They ate Chinese food and Jimmy discussed ministry and NASCAR. Jon passed the interview and in June 2004 Jon became the Minister of Students. This staff hire was the last full-time ministry staffing change until Jimmy's retirement. Jimmy, Jim, and Jon served from 2004 – 2016 as a ministry team.

Jon grew the youth group and led the college ministry on mission trips to Mexico, France, and

Ireland. Jon continued his studies by attending the Birmingham Extension of New Orleans Baptist Theological Seminary. He graduated in 2008 with his Master of Divinity.

Faith & Katrina

When I study our church records, I often come across church members initially reached through Faith evangelism. Pioneered by Bobby Welch at FBC Daytona, FL, Faith is a 16-week program that equips church members for visitation and evangelism. Jimmy and Jim traveled to Montgomery AL to be the first in the State trained in this new program.

They completed the 16-week training in two days and returned with a desire to see Faith implemented at Skyland. Skyland participated in Faith for 12 semesters, with over 60 people of all ages participating. The group met for a short bible study and then left for visitation. Each Sunday, church members were invited to write down prospects who were visited the following week. This ministry brought the church together in service and introduced many new people to Christ and Skyland Baptist Church.

In August 2005 when I was in High School, I remember watching the horrific scenes develop in New Orleans, LA in the aftermath of Hurricane Katrina. Little did I know but many miles away Skyland sprang into action to care for those displaced by the hurricane.

Skyland was a registered Red Cross Relief Center and hosted thousands of people as they escaped the flood waters of New Orleans. When I first arrived, there were still Sunday School rooms filled with cot's, coolers, and hand sanitizers from those relief efforts. The Red Cross recognized Skyland for their service and the award they gave Skyland currently resides on Jon's bookshelf.

The Jimmy Interviews

Jimmy continued to serve faithfully as pastor and The Alabama Baptist interviewed him in 2011 and 2014. Below are excerpts from the articles.

Someone You Should Know

Skyland Boulevard Baptist Church, Tuscaloosa[26]
Tuscaloosa Baptist Association
Favorite Bible Verse: Hebrews 13:6
Favorite Hymn: "Amazing Grace"
Hobbies: Spending time with grandson
Family Status: Married to Nancy Carolyn for 52
years, one daughter and one grandson

Jimmy Garner has served as pastor of Skyland
Boulevard Baptist Church, Tuscaloosa, for nearly 22
years.

Q: How did you become a Christian?
A: I was a member at Woodville Baptist Church near
Huntsville, but I wasn't saved. Because of the
faithfulness of the ministry of that church and the
Lord touching my heart, I accepted Christ at the age
of 38.

Q: What led you to become a pastor?
A: After I was saved in 1975, two years later, I felt in
my heart God was calling me and I couldn't get away
from that and I surrendered. I began preaching in
1979.

---

[26]Someone you Should Know. *The Alabama
Baptist Newspaper:* March 10th 2011.

Q: Why have you continued serve as a pastor?
A: I have stayed because when I surrendered to the ministry, I knew that was what God wanted me to do for the rest of my life. I wouldn't be happy doing anything else.

Q: What have you gotten from serving in the ministry?
A: It has meant fulfillment in my life and contentment. It's a joy to know I'm doing what He has called me to do.

Q: How do family members support you?
A: My wife, daughter, son-in-law and grandson all are believers and support me in prayer.

Q: How do you see yourself involved in the ministry in the future?
A: I don't have any plans now of retirement. I want to pastor as long as I can effectively serve the church and serve my people.

Skyland Boulevard Pastor Garner Marks 25 Years

Jimmy Garner celebrated his 25-year anniversary as pastor of Skyland Boulevard Baptist Church, Tuscaloosa, with a reception and special service Aug. 3. "It's been a great joy to be able to serve a congregation for 25 years," Garner said. Prior to

Skyland Boulevard Baptist he served as pastor of Open Acres Baptist Church, Montgomery; Hollywood Baptist Church; and Bethany Baptist Church, Section. He also served as minister of education and evangelism at a church in Mississippi. While he has loved serving churches, Garner never expected that his career path would include the role of pastor. Garner accepted Christ at the age of 38 while he was working in the sales industry.

By the age of 40, he had accepted the call into ministry despite being two years shy of retiring from his sales job. "The only thing that mattered to me is to do what the Lord wanted me to do," Garner said of the career change. To celebrate the anniversary Aug. 3, Skyland Boulevard held a reception at 3:30 p.m. as a time of fellowship with light refreshments and a celebration service at 6 p.m. Members from Garner's previous churches, as well as family from Tennessee, gathered with the Skyland Boulevard church family to honor him.

The service was filled with testimonies and stories of Garner's impact in participants' lives. As a gift, the church is giving him a nine-week sabbatical. Garner plans to use the time to refresh and evaluate his ministry. He said a sabbatical is "one of the best things a church can do for a pastor." Garner and his wife of 56 years, Carolyn, have one daughter and one grandson.[27]

The Second Retirement

In the summer of 2015, Jimmy approached Jon and discussed the need for a part-time assistant Student Pastor to help with Middle School ministry. Although this was to help with the immediate ministry, there was another thought in Jimmy's mind.

Jimmy was starting to think about retirement and wanted to ensure the church was prepared and people in place for when he felt led by the Lord to retire. The Lord works in wonderful ways, and it was myself who Jon approached to start part-time in the youth department.

On a Wednesday morning in July 2016, Jimmy told Carolyn he was leaving to pray about his future. He returned to Woodville Baptist Church, where he had been saved all those years previously. When he

---

[27]Skyland Boulevard Pastor Garner Marks 25 Years. *The Alabama Baptist Newspaper*: September 11, 2014.

arrived, the church asked him to lead the Wednesday service. At the end of the service, Jimmy asked for a key to the Sanctuary and the following day Jimmy entered the Sanctuary at 8:30 am and began to pray. Jimmy sat in the pews, walked the aisles, and stood in the pulpit as he prayed and asked God for wisdom in what to do in his life.

The altar of Woodville Baptist was the place of many important moments in the life of Jimmy Garner and, therefore, the direction of Skyland. At 1:30 pm, after four hours of prayer and petition, Jimmy had his peace. He left the Sanctuary, drove home, and called an unscheduled deacon's meeting. Jimmy had received the peace and wisdom from the Lord that it was time to retire.

The deacons met in the gym and Jimmy stood up and announced he was retiring after 27 years of shepherding Skyland. Jimmy understood he could not choose the next pastor but asked the Deacons if Jon Wiggins would be the first candidate for consideration. On May 8th at the end of the Sunday Morning service, Jimmy announced to the congregation his desire to retire on August 7th 2016. After prayerful consideration, the deacon body proposed for Jon Wiggins to be the Senior Pastor and for me, Alex Cowan, to take Jon's previous position as the Student Pastor.

The Church voted in an evening service in late July 2016. Jon and I were both asked to share our testimonies and explain why we believed God was leading us to these specific roles. The congregation voted by placing an anonymous ballot into the offering plate. The deacons stepped outside to count the votes, and the choir stepped into the choir loft and led the congregation in singing. It truly is a nerve-racking moment when you are awaiting the public results of whether you passed your job interview.

The Deacons filed in the side door of the Sanctuary and Parks Burgin, the Chairman of Deacons, announced Jon and I passed the necessary threshold with vote shares of 96%. The church had now spoken and selected the next Senior Pastor and Student Pastor.

The Church Clerk Judy Hayes, recorded the minutes of this meeting on Sunday May 22nd at 6:00pm. Hayes recorded,

"The deacon body gave a unified recommendation for both men for their perspective position and secret ballots were distributed to all SBBC members in attendance. Mr. Burgin presented a motion to call Rev. Jon Wiggins to be Pastor of SBBC. The motion was seconded by Nick Lolley. There was a call for discussion; there was none. Mr. Burgin then presented a motion to call Alex Cowan to be full-time Student Minister at SBBC. The motion was seconded by Dennis James. Mr. Burgin called for discussion; none voiced. Mr. Burgin then explained the ballot process and instructed members to mark the ballots "Yes" or "No" for each man/position for which they have been presented. Following collection and counting of ballots by members of the Deacon body, Mr. Burgin announced that the call for Rev. Jon Wiggins as Pastor and Alex Cowan as Student Minister were each affirmed by 96% of the vote. A motion to destroy the ballots was made by Jerry Mimms, seconded by Dennis James. The motion passed. Mr. Burgin made a motion to adjourn the meeting; Jerry Mims seconded and the motion carried. In dismissal, those present stood demonstrating unanimous support for the decisions made in this meeting." [28]

---

[28]Minutes, Special Called Business Meeting. Sunday May 22nd 2016, 6:00pm.

Quickly, August 7th arrived, and Jimmy preached his last Sunday Morning Service. The Evening Service had a strange feeling in the air. It felt similar to your High School Graduation, where there is excitement about the future but also an understanding that the way things have always been will no longer be.

At the end of the Evening Service, Jimmy passed the shepherd's crook to Jon. This physical symbol illustrated the spiritual handover from one shepherd to another. As Jimmy stepped out of the pulpit for the last time, a prosperous era of our church ended. And a new chapter in the history of Skyland was about to begin.

Church Staff

Carolyn Hatfield
Financial Secretary

Glenda Roberts
Secretary

Mike Bennett
Children's Director

Julia Terry
Pianist

Ray Gibson
Organist

Cathy Watkins
Nursery Worker

Church Support Staff, 2008

FAITH Team, 2000

Pastor Jimmy Garner, 2000

Bro. Jimmy and Jon, 2004

Jon with youth, 2004

Bro. Jimmy teaching VBS, 2004

Pastor Jimmy's last service

Jim Young
Assoc. Pastor/Ed/Music

Jason Walker
Youth Director

Ministerial Staff, 2000

CHAPTER FIVE
CONCLUSION

Jon Wiggins became only the third senior pastor in 53 years of Skyland history. This pastoral longevity has as much to do with the sheep as it has to do with the shepherds. The congregation at 3320 Skyland Boulevard East has shown within the pages of this book to have a propensity to love God, their church, and their pastors abundantly.

I am writing this book in the spring of 2023 in preparation for our church's 60th anniversary. Jon has served for seven years as Senior Pastor, and I currently serve as our Associate Pastor with Josh Hill (Worship) and Ian Bennett (Students) Jim Young (Senior Adults) and Niki Olek (Preschool). Jimmy is still preaching at local churches and winning people to the Lord.

Skyland has weathered the pastoral transition well and is growing from strength to strength. The Coronavirus Pandemic had its difficulties, but the Lord showed His gracious mercy throughout. I hope to write an updated history chronicling these events in years to come. It is the duty of all generations to tell their story of God's faithfulness and may we not shirk from that responsibly.

As we conclude, may we always be thankful that at Skyland, we do indeed stand on the shoulders of giants. To all past members, deacons, and to Jerome and Jimmy, thank you for your faithfulness. You have set an example for future generations, and may we strive to build upon the foundation which you have laid.

To God be the glory,

Alex Cowan

Jude 24-25

Church Staff, 2023

Jon and Bro. Jimmy, 2023
Jimmy is receiving an advance copy of this book.

Made in the USA
Columbia, SC
18 May 2023

16905697R10053